Warren,

so sweet the dance and the
desire to linger.

Linda

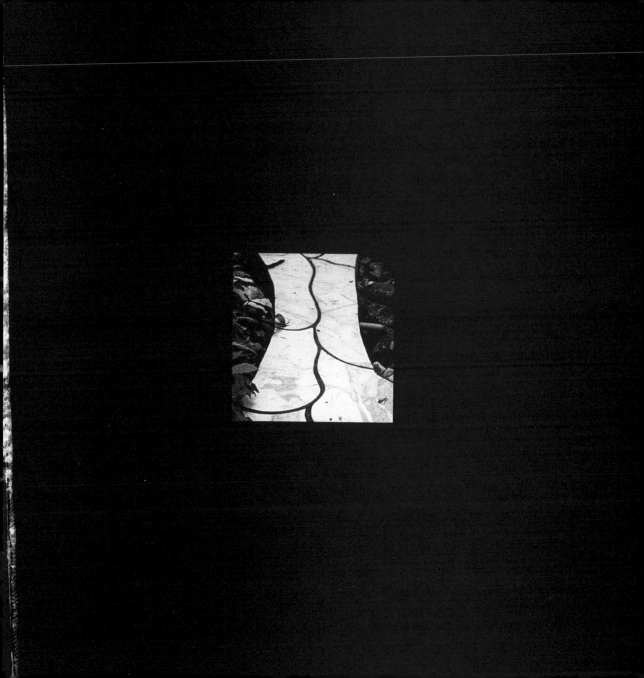

YOUR
ANSWERS
QUESTIONED

YOUR
ANSWERS
QUESTIONED

Explorations for Open Minds

OSHO

St. Martin's Press ❧ New York

www.stmartins.com

Book design by pink design, inc. (www.pinkdesigninc.com)

ISBN 0-312-32077-9

First Edition: September 2003

10 9 8 7 6 5 4 3 2 1

AN INTRODUCTION

In a classic performance piece written by Jane Wagner and performed by Lily Tomlin, the delightful character Trudy informs her audience that she is, in the company of her friends from outer space, "In Search of Intelligent Life in the Universe." Trudy is a bag lady, and she challenges our assumptions about what is crazy and what is sane; what is true, and what is just the acquired habit of years of trying to adapt ourselves to a world full of falsities. "I got the kind of madness Socrates talks about," she explains. "A divine release of the soul from the yoke of custom and convention."

That "release of the soul from the yoke of custom and convention" is precisely what this little book aims to provoke in its readers. Or, if you don't like the religious flavor of the word "soul," you can define it as the release of the intelligence and clarity that each of us brought into the world when we were born. That quality of wonder and spontaneity that makes all children so beautiful, and when it is absent in adults makes them seem so dreary and sad.

A story:

For a couple of years I lived and worked in London. The English have this wonderful way of packing whole landscapes into tiny squares of earth in front of their row houses, and their climate blesses them with a spring that seems to last forever. My first London spring, I used to walk each morning to the train that took me to work. Past all the gardens, through heaps of blossoms on the sidewalk after a rain, and each morning it seemed there was something new in each garden.

At one house, my passage almost always coincided with what I took to be "leaving for kindergarten" time for a mother and her small daughter. Their garden was a particularly beautiful one, and along one side grew an abundance of hydrangeas. I had been watching as the flowers slowly unfolded and began, day by day, to turn

from green to lighter green to just a hint of pink. And on this one morning, after a rare full day of sunshine the day before, they had all burst into full color. The overnight transformation was breathtaking, and just as I came even with the house I heard the little girl say, "Mummy!! Mummy, look!!!" and I knew she had seen them too. Her mother said slowly, precisely, in the way one teaches a child, "Yes dear. Those are *hy-dran-geas.*"

During the rest of my walk to the train station, this little exchange hung in my thoughts. Would this small girl's mind forever associate the word *hydrangea* with moments of wonder and beauty? Faced with her first awesome sunset at the beach, the first stirrings of romance in her heart, would she say to herself, "It's just so...so *hydrangea*"? I couldn't figure out whether to laugh or cry. This has happened to all of us in so many ways, this transformation from child full of wonder to adult full of answers...often to questions we haven't even asked. We learn to label things, to compare and categorize them—"hydrangea"—to add them to an increasingly heavy yoke of customary answers and conventions, and set about to collect more.

Not to say that answers aren't useful sometimes. They are. But when they pile up unquestioned for years—for generations, centuries, even—well, it's clear what a mess that's got us into.

In her search for intelligent life in the universe, Trudy tells us that she's discovered that "the human mind is kind of like a piñata. When you break it open, you find all kinds of surprises inside."

The premise of this book is that your answers form the shell of your own individual piñata. And if you can take the risk of breaking it open—not in order to substitute new answers for the old ones but to clear a space and let the breezes blow through—you just might find, as Trudy has found, that "losing your mind can be a peak experience!"

Carol Neiman

YOUR

ANSWERS

QUESTIONED

ARE YOU READY?

The less people know, the more stubbornly they know it. ▨

The intelligent person hesitates, ponders, wavers. The unintelligent never wavers, never hesitates. Where the wise will whisper, the fool simply declares from the housetops. ▦

"The truth" is only a way of speaking; there is not something labeled "truth" such that one day you will find and open the box and see the contents and say, "Great! I have found the truth." There is no such box. Your *existence* is the truth, and when you are silent you are *in* truth. And if the silence is absolute then you are the ultimate truth.

But don't think of the truth as an object—it is not an object. It is not *there*, it is *here*. ▣

Each day brings its own problems, its own challenges and each moment brings its own questions. And if you have ready-made answers in your head you will not be able even to listen to the question. You will be so full of your answer, you will be incapable of listening. You will not be available. ▦

Many of our problems—perhaps most of our problems—are because we have never looked at them face-to-face, encountered them. And not looking at them is giving them energy. Being afraid of them is giving them energy, always trying to avoid them is giving them energy— because you are accepting that they are real. Your very acceptance is their existence. Other than your acceptance, they don't exist. ▦

There has never been a person like you before, there is nobody else like you right now in the whole world, and there will never be anybody like you. Just see how much respect existence has paid to you. You are a masterpiece—unrepeatable, incomparable, utterly unique.

Stop judging yourself. Instead of judging, start accepting yourself with all the imperfections, all the frailties, all the mistakes, all the failures. Don't ask yourself to be perfect. That is simply asking for something impossible, and then you will feel frustrated. You are a human being, after all. ▨

Don't be bothered about perfection. Replace the word "perfection" with "totality." Don't think in terms of having to be perfect, think in terms of having to be total. Totality will give you a different dimension.

There is a tremendous difference between perfection and totality. Perfection is a goal somewhere in the future, totality is an experience in the here and now. Totality is not a goal, it is a style of life. ▨

The greatest calamity that can happen to a person is to become too serious and too practical. A little bit of craziness, a little bit of eccentricity, is all for the good. ▨

Courage means going into the unknown in spite of all the fears.
Courage does not mean fearlessness. Fearlessness happens if you go
on being courageous and more courageous. That is the ultimate
experience of courage—fearlessness. That is the fragrance of what
happens when the courage has become absolute.

But in the beginning there is not much difference between the coward
and the courageous person. The only difference is, the coward listens
to his fears and follows them, and the courageous person puts them
aside and goes ahead. The courageous person goes into the unknown
in spite of all the fears. ▨

Existence is not a problem to be solved, it is a mystery to be lived. And you should be perfectly aware what the difference is between a mystery and a problem.

A problem is something created by the mind; a mystery is something that is simply there, not created by the mind. A problem has an ugliness in it, like a disease. A mystery is beautiful. With a problem, immediately a fight arises. You have to solve it; something is wrong, you have to put it right; something is missing, you have to supply the missing link. With a mystery there is no question of that.

The moon rises in the night....It is not a problem, it is a mystery. You have to live with it. You have to dance with it, you have to sing with it, or you can just be silent with it. Something mysterious surrounds you. ▓

You go on dreaming, imagining beautiful things for the coming days, for the future. And in moments when danger is imminent, then suddenly you become aware that there may be no future, no tomorrow, that this is the only moment you have. Times of disaster are very revealing. They don't bring anything new to the world; they simply make you aware of the world as it is. They wake you up. If you don't understand this, you can go mad; if you understand it, you can become awakened. ▨

Put everything at stake. Be a gambler! Risk everything, because the next moment is not certain, so why bother? Why be concerned? Live dangerously, live joyously. Live without fear, live without guilt. Live without any fear of hell or any greed for heaven. Just live. ▣

BREAKING OUT OF THE BOX

It is good to be curious because that is how one starts the journey of inquiry into existence; but if one simply remains curious, then there will be no intensity in it. One can move from one curiosity to another—one will become a driftwood—from one wave to another wave, never getting anchored anywhere. ·

Curiosity is good as a beginning, but then one has to become more passionate. One has to make life a quest, not only a curiosity.

And what do I mean when I say one has to make one's life a quest? Questions are many, a quest is one. When some question becomes so important to you that you are ready to sacrifice your life for it, then it is a quest. When some question has such importance, such significance that you can gamble, that you can stake all that you have, then it becomes a quest. ▨

Death is secure, life is insecurity. One who really wants to live has to live in danger, in constant danger. One who wants to reach the peaks has to take the risk of getting lost. One who wants to climb the highest peaks has to take the risk of falling from somewhere, slipping down. ▨

The society teaches you, "Choose the convenient, the comfortable; choose the well-trodden path where your forefathers and their forefathers and their forefathers, since Adam and Eve, have been walking. Choose the well-trodden path. That is a proof—so many millions of people have passed on it, you cannot go wrong."

But remember one thing: The crowd has never had the experience of truth. Truth has only happened to individuals.

Whenever there are alternatives, beware: Don't choose the convenient, the comfortable, the respectable, the socially acceptable, the honorable. Choose something that rings a bell in your heart. Choose something that you would like to do in spite of any consequences. ▣

To commit mistakes is not wrong—commit as many mistakes as possible, because that is the way you will be learning more. But don't commit the same mistake again and again, because that makes you stupid. ▓

You have to save yourself from so many well-intentioned people, do-gooders, who are constantly advising you to be this, to be that. Listen to them and thank them. They don't mean any harm—but harm is what happens. Just listen to your own heart. That is your only teacher. In the real journey of life, your own intuition is your only teacher. ▒

There is something of immense importance about truth: Unless you find it, it never becomes truth to you.

If it is somebody else's truth and you borrow it, in that very borrowing it is no longer true—it has become a lie. ▦

Whatever you are doing, whatever you are thinking, whatever you are deciding, remember one thing: Is it coming from you or is somebody else speaking? And you will be surprised to find the real voice; perhaps it is your mother—you will hear her speak again. Perhaps it is your father; it is not at all difficult to detect. It remains there, recorded in you exactly as it was given to you for the first time—the advice, the order, the discipline, the commandment.

Get rid of the voices that are within you, and soon you will be surprised to hear a still, small voice which you have never heard before; you cannot decide whose voice this is. No, it is not your mother's, it is not your father's, it is not your priest's, not your teacher's...then a sudden recognition that it is *your* voice. That's why you are not able to find its identity, to whom it belongs.

Discover your voice.

Then follow it with no fear.

Wherever it leads, there is the goal of your life, there is your destiny. It is only there that you will find fulfillment, contentment.

TRUTH OR CONSEQUENCES

Don't think of consequences; only cowards think of consequences. ▣

Everybody is telling you to keep a low profile. Why? Such a small life, why keep a low profile?

Jump as high as you can.

Dance as madly as you can. ▦

To be just like everybody else means to be part of all kinds of lies the society calls etiquette, manners. The reason is clear why people talk about truth and still remain in the world of lies. There is a longing in their hearts for the truth. They are ashamed of themselves for their being untrue, so they talk about truth but it is mere talk. To live according to it is too dangerous; they cannot risk it.

And the same is the case with freedom. Everybody wants freedom as far as talking is concerned, but nobody really is free and nobody really wants to be free, because freedom brings responsibility. It does not come alone.

The difference between ambition and longing is that ambition is goal-oriented, longing is source-oriented. Ambition means there is something to achieve "out there." It depends on a goal, there is a motive; hence you can be rational about it. You can figure out whether it is worth achieving or not. It is not a question of feeling, it has to be calculated. You have to move in a certain direction cautiously, because the world is very cunning and everybody is trying to achieve the same goal and there is competition. You have to be clever and cunning, very cautious. You have to be political, diplomatic.

Longing has no goal but it has a source. The heart is the source.

Vincent van Gogh would always paint his trees so big that they would go beyond the stars. The stars would be small, the sun and moon would be small, and the trees would be so huge....Somebody asked him, "Are you mad or something? Why do you go on painting such big trees? The farthest star is millions and millions of light-years away and your trees go on reaching beyond the stars! What nonsense is this?"

And van Gogh would laugh and he would say, "I know! But I know something more, too, of which you are not aware: The trees are the longings of the earth to transcend the stars. I am painting the longing, not the trees. I am more concerned with the source, not with the goal. It is irrelevant whether they reach the stars or not. I belong to the earth, I am part of it, and I understand the longing of the earth. This is the longing of the earth expressed through the trees—to go on reaching for the stars."

And for a longing, everything is possible. Nothing is impossible, because there is no question of reaching anywhere—it is just enjoying the source of longing itself.

Look deep into your heart. Listen to the still, small voice within. And remember one thing: Life is fulfilled only through longings, never through ambitions. ▨

Life is basically insecure. That's its intrinsic quality; it cannot be changed. Death is secure, absolutely secure. The moment you choose security, unknowingly you have chosen death. The moment you choose life, unawares you have chosen insecurity.

With the secure, with the familiar you are bored; you start becoming dull. With the insecure, with the unknown, the uncharted, you feel ecstatic, beautiful, again a child—again those eyes of wonder, again that heart which can feel awe. 🀫

Who is afraid of death? I have never come across such a person.
And almost every person I have come across is afraid of life.

Drop fear of life....Because either you can be afraid or you can live;
it is up to you. And what is there to be afraid of? You can't lose
anything. You have everything to gain.

Drop all fears and jump totally into life. ▦

Be life-affirmative. Life is synonymous with god. You can drop the word "god"—life is god. Live with reverence, with great respect and gratitude. You have not earned this life, it has been a sheer gift from the beyond. Feel thankful and prayerful, and take as many bites of it as possible and chew it well and digest it well. And experience life in all possible ways—good/bad, bitter/sweet, dark/light, summer/winter. Experience all the dualities. Don't be afraid of experience, because the more experience you have, the more integrated you become. ▣

It is only the unlived past which becomes your psychological burden. Let me repeat: The unlived past—those moments which you could have lived, but you have not lived, those love affairs which could have flowered, but you missed...those songs which you could have sung, but you remained stuck to some stupid thing and missed the song—it is the unlived past which becomes your psychological burden, and it goes on becoming heavier every day.

That's why the old man becomes so irritable. It is not his fault. He does not know why he is so irritable—why everything and each thing irritates him, why he is constantly angry, why he cannot allow anybody to be happy, why he cannot see children dancing, singing, jumping, rejoicing, why he wants everybody to be quiet—what has happened to him?

It is a simple psychological phenomenon: his whole unlived life. When he sees a child start dancing his inner child hurts. His inner child was somehow prevented from dancing—perhaps by his parents, his elders, perhaps by himself because it was respected, honored. He was brought before the neighbors and introduced: "Look at this child, how quiet, calm, silent; no disturbance, no mischief." His ego was fulfilled. Anyway, he missed. Now he cannot bear it, he cannot tolerate this child. In fact it is his unlived childhood that starts hurting. It has left a wound.

And how many wounds are you carrying? Thousands of wounds are in line, because how much have you left unlived? ▩

When you are meeting a friend—meet. Who knows? You may not be meeting again. Then you will repent. Then that unfulfilled past will haunt you, that you wanted to say something and you could not say it. There are people who want to say to somebody, "I love you," and they are waiting for years and have not said it. And the person one day may die, and then they will cry and weep and they will say, "I wanted to say to the person, 'I love you,' but I could not even say that." ▨

Whatever you dream, take note of it. That dream indicates what you are missing in reality. A man who lives in reality—his dreams start disappearing. There is nothing for him to dream. By the time he goes to sleep he is finished with the work of the day. He is finished, he has no hangover that moves into dreams. ▣

The fear of death is not the fear of death, it is a fear of remaining unfulfilled. You are going to die, and nothing, nothing at all could you experience through life—no maturity, no growth, no flowering.

Empty-handed you came, empty-handed you are going. This is the fear. ▨

MAJORITY RULES

Avoid those pretenders who decide for you; take the reins in your own hands. You have to decide. In fact, in that very decisiveness, your soul is born. When others decide for you, your soul remains asleep and dull. When you start deciding on your own, a sharpness arises. ▦

Truth is not democratic. It is not to be decided by votes what is true; otherwise we could never come to any truth, ever. People will vote for what is comfortable—and lies are very comfortable because you don't have to do anything about them, you just have to believe. Truth needs great effort, discovery, risk, and it needs you to walk alone on a path that nobody has traveled before. ▦

The majority consists of fools, utter fools. Beware of the majority. If so many people are following something, that is enough proof that it is wrong. Truth happens to individuals, not to crowds. ▨

Whenever you follow your potential, you always become the best.
Whenever you go astray from the potential, you remain mediocre.
The whole society consists of mediocre people for the simple reason
that nobody is what he was destined to be—he is something else. ▧

Man is born as a seed; he can become a flower, he may not. It all depends on you, what you do with yourself; it all depends on you whether you grow or you don't. It is your choice—and each moment the choice has to be faced; each moment you are on the crossroads. ▣

MIND GAMES

Forget all about figuring out what it is. Rather, live it; rather, enjoy it! Don't analyze it, celebrate it. ▣

Your mind is always asking, "Why? For what?" And anything that has no answer to the question, "For what?" slowly, slowly becomes of no value to you. That's how love has become valueless. What point is there in love? Where is it going to lead you? What is going to be the achievement out of it? Will you attain some utopia, some paradise?

Of course, love has no point in that way.

It is pointless.

What is the point of beauty? You see a sunset—you are stunned, it is so beautiful, but any idiot can ask the question, "What is the meaning of it?" and you will be without any answer. And if there is no meaning then why unnecessarily are you bragging about beauty?

A beautiful flower, or a beautiful painting, or beautiful music, beautiful poetry—they don't have any point. They are not arguments to prove something, neither are they means to achieve any end.

And living consists only of those things which are pointless.

Let me repeat it: Living consists only of those things which have no point at all, which have no meaning at all—meaning in the sense that they don't have any goal, that they don't lead you anywhere, that you don't get anything out of them.

In other words, living is significant in itself. ▨

All that you see has been invented by playful people, not by serious people. The serious people are too past-oriented—they go on repeating the past because they know it works. They are never inventive. ▦

"Contemporary mind" is a contradiction in terms. Mind is never contemporary, it is always old. Mind is past—past and past and nothing else; mind means memory. There can be no contemporary mind; to be contemporary is to be without mind. ▣

Just look, watch. What is your mind? What is meant by the word, "mind"? What exactly does it consist of?

All your experiences, knowledge, the past, accumulated—that is your mind. You may have a materialist's mind, you may have a spiritualist's mind, it doesn't matter a bit; the mind is the mind. The spiritual mind is as much a mind as the materialist mind. And we have to go beyond the mind. ▦

From Aristotle to Wittgenstein, thousands of brilliant people have wasted their whole brilliance for the simple reason that they were trying to solve single problems rather than going to the very root of all. The mind is the only problem.

Mind knows only conflict. Even where there is no conflict, mind creates it; even where there is no problem, mind creates it.

Mind cannot exist without problems; problems are its nourishment. Conflict, fight, disharmony—and the mind is perfectly at ease and at home. Silence, harmony—and the mind starts becoming afraid, because harmony, silence, and peace are nothing but death to the mind. ▣

The mind is a robot. The robot has its utility; this is the way the mind functions. You learn something; when you learn it, in the beginning you are aware. For example, if you learn swimming you are very alert, because life is in danger. Or if you learn to drive a car you are very alert. You have to be alert. You have to be careful about many things— the steering wheel, the road, the people passing by, the accelerator, the brake, the clutch. You have to be aware of everything. There are so many things to remember, and you are nervous, and it is dangerous to commit a mistake. It is so dangerous, that's why you have to keep aware. But the moment you have learned driving, this awareness will not be needed. Then the robot part of your mind will take it over.

That's what we call learning. Learning something means it has been transferred from consciousness to the robot. That's what learning is all about. Once you have learned a thing it is no longer part of the conscious mind—it has been delivered to the unconscious. Now the unconscious can do it; now your consciousness is free to learn something else.

This is in itself tremendously significant. Otherwise you will remain learning a single thing your whole life.

The mind is a great servant, a great computer. Use it, but remember that it should not overpower you. Remember that you should remain capable of being aware, that it should not possess you in toto, that it should not become all and all, that a door should be left open from where you can come out of the robot. ▣

Don't reject the mind—understand it.

When you understand something you go beyond it; it is below you. The mind has its utility—a great utility. There will be no science without the mind, no technology. All human comforts will disappear without the human mind. Man will fall back into the world of the animals, or even far below the animals, without the mind. The mind has given much.

The problem is not the mind; the problem is your identification with it. You think you *are* it, that is the problem.

Disidentify. You be the watcher and let the mind be there—watched, witnessed, observed. And a great radical change happens through observation. The mind functions far more efficiently when you observe it because all that is rubbish drops and the mind need not carry unnecessary weight; it becomes light. And when you become a watcher, the mind can have some rest too. Otherwise your whole life the mind is working, working, day in, day out, year in, year out; it stops only when you die. It creates a deep fatigue, mental fatigue.

Now scientists say even metals become tired—there is a thing called metal fatigue. So what to say about the mind, which is very subtle, which is very delicate? Handle it carefully. But you remain aloof, unconcerned, uninvolved. When you are writing you don't become the fountain pen, although you cannot write without it. A good fountain pen is essential for good writing. If you start writing with your fingers nobody will be able to read what you have written, not even you, and it will be very primitive. But you are not the fountain pen, and the fountain pen is not the writer but only a writing instrument.

The mind is not the master but only an instrument in the hands of the master. ▩

To train the mind for concentration is very difficult, because it goes on revolting, it goes on falling back into its old habits. You pull it again, and it escapes. You bring it again to the subject you were concentrating on and suddenly you find you are thinking of something else, you have forgotten what you are concentrating upon. It is not an easy job.

But to put it aside is a very simple thing—not difficult at all. All that you have to do is to watch. Whatsoever is going on in your mind, don't interfere, don't try to stop it. Do not do anything, because whatsoever you do will become a discipline.

So do not do anything at all. Just watch.

The strangest thing about the mind is that if you become a watcher, it starts disappearing. Just like the light disperses darkness, watchfulness disperses the mind, its thoughts, its whole paraphernalia. ▣

Intellect is thinking—consciousness is discovered in a state of no-thinking, so utterly silent that not even a single thought moves as a disturbance. In that silence you discover your very being—it is as vast as the sky. And to know it is really to know something worthwhile; otherwise all your knowledge is garbage. Your knowledge may be useful, utilitarian, but it is not going to help you transform your being. It cannot bring you to a fulfillment, to contentment, to enlightenment, to a point where you can say, "I have come home." ▨

Your thoughts are not you. There is a constant traffic. On the screen of the mind so many thoughts are moving, but you are not one of them. You are a witness, you are outside; you are seeing those thoughts moving.

Anything that you can see is not you. That should be the criterion: Anything you can witness is not you. You are the witness. ▦

IN LOVE

The head says, "Think before you jump." And the heart says, "Jump before you think." Their ways are diametrically opposite. Love is jumping into a dangerously alive situation with no calculation beforehand. ▪

Each person is such an infinite mystery, inexhaustible, unfathomable, that it is not possible that you can ever say, "I have known her," or, "I have known him." At the most you can say, "I have tried my best, but the mystery remains a mystery." In fact, the more you know, the more mysterious the other becomes. Then love is a constant adventure.

How can you know the other? You can love, and through love this miracle happens. If you love the other, great understanding arises on its own. Not that you try to understand the other: You simply love the other as he or she is, with no judgment. ▣

Real love is not an escape from loneliness, real love is an overflowing aloneness. One is so happy in being alone that one would like to share. Happiness always wants to share. It is too much, it cannot be contained, like the flower cannot contain its fragrance—it has to be released. ▦

Loneliness is where you are missing the other.

Aloneness is when you are finding yourself. ▣

Love is a by-product of freedom; it is the overflowing joy of freedom, it is the fragrance of freedom. First the freedom has to be there, then love follows. ▨

Mind is good where money is concerned, mind is good where war is concerned, mind is good where ambitions are concerned, but mind is absolutely useless when love is concerned. Money, war, desire, ambitions—you cannot put love in the same category. Love has a separate source in your being. ▦

Love is the only commandment. If love is not there, then even the Ten Commandments are not going to help at all. Ten commandments are not needed; they are needed only because you are not ready to fulfill the first and the only commandment. Those Ten Commandments are just poor substitutes for the single commandment: love.

THE MORNING AFTER

There are old stories of frogs becoming beautiful princes. In my own experience just the opposite happens: You bring home a beautiful prince and overnight, in the morning, you find there is a frog. ▣

The problems of jealousy and possessiveness are not really problems but symptoms, symptoms that you don't yet know what love is. We take it for granted that we know what love is, and then the problem of jealousy arises. That is not right. The problem is arising because love is not yet there; it simply shows that love has not yet arrived, it simply shows the absence of love. So you cannot solve it.

All that is needed is to forget about jealousy, because that is a negative fight. It is fighting with darkness; it is pointless. Rather, light a candle. That's what love is. Once love starts flowing, jealousy and possessiveness become nonexistent. You are simply surprised at where they have gone, you cannot find them. It is just as when you light a candle, you can go on looking for darkness all over the room and you will not find it. You are even looking with a light and you cannot find it. You cannot find it with light because it is no longer there; it was simply an absence of light. Jealousy is the absence of love.

Before you can relate with somebody else, relate with yourself: that is the basic requirement to be fulfilled. Without it, nothing is possible. With it, nothing is impossible. ▣

Millions of people are suffering: They want to be loved but they don't know how to love. And love cannot exist as a monologue; it is a dialogue, a very harmonious dialogue. ▦

Drop these ideas of being men and women; we are all human beings. To be a man or a woman is a very superficial thing. Don't make much fuss about it. It is not anything very important; don't make it a big deal. ▒

Live and love, and love totally and intensely—but never against freedom. Freedom should remain the ultimate value. ▦

WHOLEHEARTED

The heart is still primitive. And it is good that the universities have not yet found a way to teach the heart and make it civilized. That is the only hope for humanity to survive. ▨

Don't condemn sensuality. It has been condemned by the whole world, and because of their condemnation, the energy that could flower into sensuality moves into perversions, jealousy, anger, hatred—a kind of life which is dry, with no juice.

Sensuousness is one of the greatest blessings to humanity. It is your sensitivity, it is your consciousness. It is your consciousness filtering through the body. ▩

The mind is not separate from your body—it is the inner part of the body. You are separate from the body and the mind, both. You are a transcendental entity; you are a witness to the mind and the body both. But your mind and your body are one and the same energy. The body is visible mind, and the mind is invisible body. The body is the exterior mind, and the mind is the interior body. ▨

Sex is a natural desire, and is good in its own place. But one should not stop with it; it is only a beginning, a glimpse—a glimpse of the beyond. In deep sexual orgasm, you become aware for the first time of something which is not of the ego, of something which is not of the mind, of something which is not of time. In deep orgasm, mind, time, everything disappears; the whole world stops for a moment. For a moment you are no longer part of the material world; you are just a pure space.

But this is only a glimpse—move ahead. Seek and search for ways and means so that this glimpse becomes your very state. That's what I call realization, enlightenment. An enlightened person is in a state of orgasmic joy twenty-four hours a day.

Orgasm is nature's indication that you contain within yourself a tremendous amount of blissfulness. It simply gives you a taste of it—then you can go on the search. ▦

Sex creates jealousy, but it is a secondary thing. So it is not a question of how to drop jealousy; you cannot drop it because you cannot drop sex. The question is how to transform sex into love, then jealousy disappears.

If you love a person, the very love is enough guarantee, the very love is enough security.

If you love a person, you know he cannot go to anybody else. And if he goes, he goes; nothing can be done. What can you do? You can kill the person, but a dead person will not be of much use.

When you love a person you trust that he cannot go to anybody else. If he goes, there is no love and nothing can be done. Love brings this understanding. There is no jealousy.

So if jealousy is there, know well there is no love. You are playing a game, you are hiding sex behind love. Love is just a painted word and the reality is sex. ▦

Jealousy is one of the most prevalent areas of psychological ignorance—about yourself, about others, and more particularly, about relationships. People think they know what love is—they do not know. And their misunderstanding about love creates jealousy.

By "love" people mean a certain kind of monopoly, some possessiveness—without understanding a simple fact of life: That the moment you possess a living being you have killed them.

Life cannot be possessed.

You cannot have it in your fist.

If you want to have it, you have to keep your hands open. ▩

What makes you jealous?

Jealousy itself is not the root.
You love a woman, you love a man; you want to possess the man or the woman just out of fear that perhaps tomorrow they may move with somebody else. The fear of tomorrow destroys your today, and it is a vicious circle.

If every day is destroyed because of the fear of tomorrow, sooner or later the man is going to look for some other woman, the woman is going to look for some other man, because you are just a pain in the neck.

And when he starts looking for another woman or she starts moving with another man, you think your jealousy has proved to be right. In fact it is your jealousy that has created the whole thing. ▓

Jealousy is comparison. And we have been taught to compare, we have been conditioned to compare, always compare. Somebody else has a better house, somebody else has a more beautiful body, somebody else has more money, somebody else has a more charismatic personality. Compare, go on comparing yourself with everybody else you pass by, and great jealousy will be the outcome; it is the by-product of the conditioning for comparison.

Otherwise, if you drop comparing, jealousy disappears. Then you simply know you are you, and you are nobody else, and there is no need. ✦

Don't be bothered about tomorrows; today is enough. Somebody loves you...let this be a day of joy, a day of celebration. Be so totally in love today that your totality and your love will be enough for the other person not to move away from you. Your jealousy will move him away; only your love can keep him with you. His jealousy will move you away; his love can keep you with him.

Don't think of tomorrow. The moment you think of tomorrow your living today remains halfhearted. Just live today, and leave tomorrow alone; it will take its own course. And remember one thing—that if today has been such a beauty of experience, such a blessing...out of today is born tomorrow, so why be worried about it? ▦

AT HOME

There is no home, unless we find it in ourselves.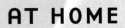

You come into this world absolutely like a plain, unwritten, open book.

You have to write your fate; there is nobody who is writing your fate.
And who will write your fate? And how? And for what?

You come into the world just an open potentiality, a multidimensional potentiality.

You have to write your fate, you have to create your destiny. You have to become yourself.

You are not born with a ready-made self. You are born only as a seed—and you can die also only as a seed, but you can become a flower, can become a tree.

Life consists of very small things. So if you become interested in so-called big things, you will be missing life.

Life consists of sipping a cup of tea, gossiping with a friend; going for a morning walk, not going anywhere in particular, just for a walk, no goal, no end, from any point you can turn back; cooking food for someone you love; cooking food for yourself, because you love your body too; washing your clothes, cleaning the floor, watering the garden—these small things, very small things—saying hello to a stranger, which was not needed at all because there was no question of any business with the stranger.

The person who can say hello to a stranger can also say hello to a flower, can also say hello to a tree, can sing a song to the birds. ▦

People have judged you, and you have accepted their idea without scrutiny. You are suffering from all kinds of people's judgments, and you are throwing those judgments on other people. This game has got out of all proportion, and the whole of humanity is suffering from it. If you want to get out of it, the first thing is: Don't judge yourself. Accept humbly your imperfection, your failures, your mistakes, your frailties. Just be yourself. There is no need to pretend that you are otherwise.

Once you accept yourself, you will be able to accept others because you will have a clear insight that they are suffering from the same disease. And your accepting of them will help them to accept themselves. If the whole of humanity comes to a point where everybody is accepted as he is, almost 90 percent of misery will simply disappear. ▣

THIN-SKINNED

Scratch a little, and in your saint you will find the sinner. ▨

If you practice a virtue it is no longer a virtue. A practiced virtue is a dead thing, a dead weight. Virtue is virtue only when it is spontaneous; virtue is virtue only when it is natural, unpracticed—when it comes out of your vision, out of your awareness, out of your understanding.

Ordinarily, religion is thought of as a practice. It is not. That is one of the most fundamental misunderstandings about religion. You can practice nonviolence but you will still remain violent, because your vision has not changed. You still carry the old eyes. A greedy person can practice sharing, but the greed will remain the same. Even the sharing will be corrupted by the greed, because you cannot practice anything against your understanding, beyond your understanding. You cannot force your life into principles unless those principles are of your own experience.

But so-called religious people try to practice virtue—that's why they are the most unvirtuous people on the earth. They try to practice love and they are the most unloving people on the earth. They have created all sorts of mischief: wars, hatred, anger, enmity, murder. They practice friendship but the friendship has not flowered on the earth. They go on talking about God but they create more and more conflict in the name of God. ▒

The only authentic responsibility is toward your own potential, your own intelligence and awareness—and to act accordingly. Values should not be imposed on you. They should grow with your awareness, in you. ▣

There are two words to be remembered: one is *reaction* and one is *response*. Most people react, they don't respond. Reaction comes from your memory, from your past experiences, from your knowledge; it is always inadequate in a fresh, new situation. And existence is continuously fresh.

So if you act according to your past, that is reaction. But that reaction is not going to change the situation, it is not going to change you, and it will lead to failure.

Response is moment to moment. It has nothing to do with memory, it has something to do with your awareness. You see the situation with clarity; you are clean, silent, serene. Out of this serenity, you act spontaneously. It is not *re*-action, it is *action*. You have never done it before. And the beauty of it is that it will suit the situation. ▨

Have a goal, and sooner or later you will end up on the psychoanalyst's couch. My vision is that of a goalless life. That is the vision of all the buddhas. Everything simply is, for no reason at all. Everything simply is utterly absurd. If this is understood, then where is the hurry, and for what? ▣

The really egoless person is not humble at all. He is neither arrogant nor humble; he is simply himself. ▦

IMMEDIATE AND ULTIMATE

The greatest obsession that humanity suffers from is of "that which should be." It is a kind of madness. The really healthy person has no concern with that which should be. His whole concern is the immediate, that which is. And you will be surprised: If you enter into the immediate, you will find the ultimate in it. If you move into that which is close by, you will find all the distant stars in it. If you move in the present moment, the whole eternity is in your hands.

Man is the only animal who is imperfect. Dogs are not imperfect, each and every dog is a perfect dog. Cats are not imperfect, trees are not imperfect, rocks are not imperfect. In this whole vast existence man is the only animal who is imperfect. And that is where his glory is— because in imperfection there is growth, in imperfection there is opening, there is evolution. When you are perfect there is nowhere to go. Perfection will be suicide for humanity.

Just think, what will you do when you are perfect? In the first place it cannot happen. In the second place, if it happens, what will you do then? The perfectionist will be at a loss, utterly at a loss, because he knows only one way of life and that is to go on improving. ▣

LAWN CARE

Everybody is wearing masks that are smiling, happy looking, and everybody is deceiving everybody else.

You wear a mask, so others think you are happier than they are, and you think others are happier than you are. The grass looks greener on the other side of the fence. They see your grass and it looks greener. It *really* looks greener, thicker, better; that is the illusion that distance creates.

Just be yourself, and then there is no misery and no competition and no worrying that others have more, or that you don't have enough. If you want the grass to be greener, there is no need to look on the other side of the fence; make the grass greener on your side of the fence! It is such a simple thing. ▨

If one really wants to live life in all its richness, one has to learn how to be inconsistent, how to be consistently inconsistent. How to be able to move from one extreme to another—sometimes rooted deep in the earth and sometimes flying high in heaven, sometimes making love and sometimes meditating. And then, slowly, your heaven and your earth will come closer and closer, and you will become the horizon where they meet. ▦

You see people who are miserable because they have compromised on every point, and they cannot forgive themselves because they have compromised. They know that they could have dared, but they proved to be cowards. In their own eyes they have fallen, they have lost self-respect. That's what compromise does.

Why should one compromise? What have we got to lose? In this small life, live as totally as possible. Don't be afraid of going to the extreme. You cannot be more than total—that is the last frontier. And don't compromise. Compromise is one of the ugliest words in the language. It means, "I give half, you give half; I settle for half, you settle for half." But why? When you can have the whole, when you can have the cake and eat it too, then why compromise? ▣

Habits can be dropped not by fighting against them. That's what people ordinarily do. If they want to change a habit they create another habit against it to fight with it. They move from one habit into another habit. If you want to drop smoking you start chewing gum; now it is as foolish as the other. You exchange one habit for another, but you remain the same unconscious person.

To drop the habit and not compensate for it, and to remain utterly aware and alert so that you don't start moving into another substitute, is one of the hardest things in life. But it is not impossible.

Real life has to be lived without habits. You have heard, again and again you have been told, "Drop bad habits." I tell you: Drop habit as such! There are not good and bad habits, all habits are bad. Remain without habits, live without habits; then you live moment-to-moment in freedom. ▣

When you have seen a little glimpse that you are the creator of your own misery, it will be very difficult for you now to go on creating it. It is easy to live in misery when you know others are creating it—what can you do? You are helpless. That's why we go on throwing responsibilities on others. ▨

The ordinary mind always throws the responsibility on somebody else. It is always the other who is making you suffer. Your wife is making you suffer, your husband is making you suffer, your parents are making you suffer, your children are making you suffer. Or the financial structure of the society, capitalism, communism, fascism, the prevalent political ideology, the social structure. Or fate, karma, god...you name it.

People have millions of ways to shirk responsibility. But the moment you say that somebody else—x, y, z—is making you suffer, then you cannot do anything to change it. What can you do? When the society changes and communism comes and there is a classless world, then everybody will be happy, until then it is not possible. How can you be happy in a society that is poor, and how can you be happy in a society that is dominated by the capitalists? How can you be happy with a society that is bureaucratic? How can you be happy with a society that does not allow you freedom?

Excuses and excuses and excuses—excuses just to avoid one single insight, that "I am responsible for myself. Nobody else is responsible for me; it is absolutely and utterly my responsibility. Whatever I am, I am my own creation." ▦

Don't blame others. Whatsoever they are, they are. In fact, all the cunningness of the world and the trickery of the world helps you to be aware. If this world cannot help you to be aware, then what world will ever be able to make you aware, to be cautious? It is a good world—it gives you a tremendous challenge to be cautious. ▣

ADAM AND EVE

We don't need a better human being, we need a new human being. Betterment has gone on for centuries and nothing has happened. Now we don't need any better humanity—enough is enough! Now we want a totally new humanity, discontinuous with the past. We want to begin again as if we are Adam and Eve, just now expelled from the Garden of Eden. ▣

How to live longer? How to attain a kind of deathlessness? People try it in many ways. To have children is one of the ways, hence the constant urge to have children. The root of this desire to have children has nothing to do with children at all, it has something to do with death. You know you will not be able to be here forever; howsoever you try, you are going to fail, you know it, because millions have failed and nobody has ever succeeded. You are hoping against hope, so find some other way. One of the simplest ways, the most ancient way, is to have children. You will not be here but something of you, a particle of you, a cell of you, will go on living. It is a vicarious way of becoming immortal. ▦

The function of parents is not to help children to grow; they will grow without you. Your function is to support, to nourish, to help what is already growing. Don't give directions and don't give ideals. Don't tell them what is right and what is wrong—let them find it through their own experience.

Children are so intelligent. Yes, they need your guidance and they need your help—they are helpless, but they are utterly intelligent too. So the parent has to be very alert about how far to help and when to stop helping. It is good to hold your child's hand when he is learning to walk, but don't go on holding his hand for his whole life. ▦

The mysteries of existence are open only to the intelligent child, and the really intelligent person keeps his childhood alive to his last breath. He never loses it—the wonder the child feels looking at the birds, looking at the flowers, looking at the sky. Intelligence also has to be, in the same way, childlike.

Jesus is right when he says, "Unless you are born again, you will not see the kingdom of God." What he calls "God" I call "existence." But the statement is true. "Born again" means becoming a child again.

But when a mature person becomes a child again, there is a difference between the ordinary child and the reborn. The ordinary child is innocent because he is ignorant, and the reborn innocence is the greatest value in life because it is not ignorance, it is pure intelligence. ▣

Intelligence is the inborn capacity to see, to perceive. Every child is born intelligent, then made stupid by the society. We educate him in stupidity and sooner or later he graduates in stupidity.

Intelligence is a natural phenomenon—just as breathing is, just as seeing is. Intelligence is the inner seeing; it is intuitive. It has nothing to do with intellect, remember. Never confuse intellect with intelligence, they are polar opposites. Intellect is of the head; it is taught by others, it is imposed on you. You have to cultivate it. It is borrowed, it is something foreign, it is not inborn.

But intelligence is inborn. It is your very being, your very nature. All animals are intelligent. They are not intellectuals, true, but they are all intelligent. Trees are intelligent, the whole existence is intelligent, and each child born is born intelligent. Have you ever come across a child who is stupid? It is impossible! But to come across a grown-up person who is intelligent is very rare; something goes wrong in between. ▦

THE RULES

Whenever commandments are given they create difficulties for people, because by the time they are given they are already out of date. Life moves so fast; it is a dynamism, it is not static. It is not a stagnant pool, it is a Ganges, it goes on flowing. It is never the same for two consecutive moments. So one thing may be right this moment, and may not be right the next. Then what to do? The only possible thing is to make people so aware that they themselves can decide how to respond to a changing life. ▨

Once you have heard a truth it is impossible to forget it. That is one of the qualities of truth, that you don't need to remember it. The lie has to be remembered continuously; you may forget. The person habituated to lies needs a better memory than the person who is habituated to truth, because a true person has no need of memory; if you only say the truth there is no need to remember.

But if you are saying a lie, then you have to continuously remember, because you have said one lie to one person, another lie to another person, something else to somebody else. What you have said and to whom you have to categorize in your mind and keep. And whenever a question arises about a lie, you have to lie again, so it is a series. The lie does not believe in birth control.

Truth is celibate, it has no children at all! ▨

The golden rule for life is that there are no golden rules.

There cannot be. Life is so vast, so immense, so strange, mysterious, it cannot be reduced into a rule or a maxim. All maxims fall short, are too small; they cannot contain life and its living energies. Hence the golden rule is significant, that there are no golden rules.

An authentic human being does not live by rules, maxims, commandments. The authentic human being simply lives. ▨

LIFE IS A VERB

Language is created for day-to-day use, language is created for the mundane world. And as far as it goes, it is good. It is perfectly adequate for the marketplace, but as you start moving into deeper waters it becomes more and more inadequate—not only inadequate, it starts becoming utterly wrong.

For example, think of these two words—*experience* and *experiencing*. When you use the word *experience* it gives you a sense of completion, as if something has come to a full stop. In life there are no full stops. Life knows nothing of full stops; it is an ongoing process, an eternal river. The goal never arrives; it is always arriving, but it never arrives. Hence the word *experience* is not right. It gives a false notion of completion, perfection; it makes you feel as if now you have arrived. Experien*cing* is far truer.

In reference to true life all nouns are wrong, only verbs are true. When you say, "This is a tree," you are making a wrong statement existentially. Not linguistically, not grammatically, but existentially you are making a wrong statement, because the tree is not a static thing, it is growing. It is never in a state of is-ness, it is always becoming. In fact, to call it a tree is not right: it is tree-ing. A river is rivering.

If you look deeply into life, nouns start disappearing, and there are only verbs. But that will create trouble in the marketplace. You cannot say to people, "I went to the rivering," or, "This morning I saw a beautiful treeing." They will think you have gone mad! But nothing is static in life; nothing is at rest. ▦

Maturity has nothing to do with your outer life experiences. It has something to do with your inward journey, experiences of the inner. Maturity is another name for realization: You have come to the fulfillment of your potential, it has become actual. The seed has come on a long journey, and has blossomed. ▣

BELIEVE IT OR NOT

The believer is not a seeker. The believer does not want to seek, that's why he believes. The believer wants to avoid seeking, that's why he believes. The believer wants to be delivered, saved. He needs a savior, he is always in search of a messiah—somebody who can eat for him, chew for him, digest for him.

But if I eat, your hunger is not going to be satisfied. Nobody can save you except yourself. ▦

Belief has nothing to do with truth. You can believe that it is night but just by your believing, it is not going to become night. You are living in a kind of hallucination.

There is this danger in belief: It makes you feel that you know the truth. And because it makes you feel that you know the truth, this becomes the greatest barrier in the search. Believe or disbelieve and you are blocked—because disbelief is also nothing but belief in a negative form.

The Catholic believes in God, the communist believes in no-God: Both are believers. Go to Kaaba or go to the Comintern, go to Kailash or to the Kremlin, it is all the same. The believer believes it is so, the nonbeliever believes it is not so. And because both have already settled, without taking the trouble to go and discover it, the stronger is their belief the greater is the barrier. They will never go on a pilgrimage, there is no point. They will live surrounded by their own illusion, self-created, self-sustained. It may be consoling, but it is not liberating. Millions of people are wasting their lives in belief and disbelief.

The inquiry into truth begins only when you drop all believing. You say, "I would like to encounter the truth on my own. I will not believe in Christ and I will not believe in Buddha. I would like to become a christ or a buddha myself, I would like to be a light unto myself." Why should one be a Christian? It is ugly. Be a christ if you can be, but don't be a Christian. Be a buddha if you have any respect for yourself, but don't be a Buddhist. The Buddhist believes. Buddha knows.

When you can know, when knowing is possible, why settle for believing? 🔳

You have to understand these two words: conscience and consciousness.

Consciousness is yours.

Conscience is given by the society, it is an imposition over your consciousness.

Different societies impose different ideas over your consciousness, but they all impose something or other. And once something is imposed over your consciousness, you cannot hear it; it is far away. Between your consciousness and you stands a thick wall of conscience that the society has imposed on you from your very childhood. ▨

Unless you make a person feel guilty, you cannot enslave him psychologically. It is impossible to imprison him in a certain ideology, a certain belief system.

But once you have created guilt in his mind, you have taken all that is courageous in him. You have destroyed all that is adventurous in him. You have repressed all possibility of his ever being an individual in his own right.

With the idea of guilt, you have almost murdered the human potential in him. He can never be independent. The guilt will force him to be dependent on a messiah, on a religious teaching, on God, on the concepts of heaven and hell, and the whole lot.

And to create guilt, all that you need is a very simple thing: Start calling mistakes, errors—sins. ▨

YES AND NO

Disobedience is a great revolution. It does not mean saying an absolute no in every situation. It simply means *deciding* whether to do it or not, whether it is beneficial to do something or not. It is taking the responsibility on yourself.

It is not a question of hating the person, or hating to be told what to do, because in that hating you cannot act obediently or disobediently; instead, you act unconsciously. You cannot act intelligently.

When you are told to do something, you are given an opportunity to respond. Perhaps what is being asked of you is right; then do it and be grateful to the person who told you at the right moment to do it. Perhaps it is not right—then make it clear. Bring your reasons, explain why it is not right; then help the person to understand that what he is thinking is going in a wrong direction. But hate has no place.

If it is right, do it lovingly. If it is not right, then even more love is needed because you will have to tell the person, explain to the person that it is not right.

The way of disobedience is not stagnant, just going against every order and feeling anger and hate and revenge toward the other person. The way of disobedience is a way of great intelligence. ▦

What is my definition of right? That which is harmonious with existence is right, and that which is disharmonious with existence is wrong. You will have to be very alert each moment, because it has to be decided each moment afresh. You cannot depend on readymade answers for what is right and what is wrong. ▓

It takes time to grow up, to mature, to come to such a maturity where you can say yes and yet remain free, where you can say yes and yet remain unique, where you can say yes and yet not become a slave.

The freedom that is brought by saying no is a very childish freedom. It is good for seven-year-olds up to fourteen-year-olds. But if a person gets caught in it and his whole life becomes a no-saying, then he has stopped growing.

The ultimate growth is to say yes with such joy as a child says no. That is a second childhood. And the one who can say yes with tremendous freedom and joy—with no hesitation, with no strings attached, with no conditions, a pure and simple joy, a pure and simple yes—that person has become a sage. That person lives in harmony again.

And this harmony is of a totally different dimension than the harmony of trees, animals, and birds. They live in harmony because they cannot say no, and the sage lives in harmony because he does not say no. Between the two, the birds and the buddhas, are all human beings— ungrown-up, immature, childish, stuck somewhere, still trying to say no to have some feeling of freedom. ▣

LIVING WITH THE DEVIL

The English word *devil* is very beautiful. If you read it backward it becomes *lived*. That which is lived becomes divine, and that which is not lived becomes the devil. Only the lived is transformed into godliness; the unlived turns poisonous. Today you postpone, and whatsoever remains unlived in you will hang around you like a weight. If you had lived it, you would have been free of it. ▨

The earth is beautiful. If you start living its beauty, enjoying its joys with no guilt in your heart, you are in paradise. If you condemn everything, every small joy, if you become a condemner, a poisoner, then the same earth turns into a hell—but only for you. It depends on you where you live, it is a question of your own inner transformation. It is not a change of place, it is a change of inner space. ▨

Let this fundamental be remembered always: If you fight with anything false, you will be defeated. The false cannot be defeated because it is false! How can you defeat something that is non-existential? There is no way. The only way is to bring light and see what is there. ▨

Life should be surrounded by love, not by fear. It is fear that creates anger. It is fear that ultimately creates violence. Have you watched? Fear is only a feminine form of anger and anger is a masculine form of fear. Fear is a passive form of anger and anger is an active form of fear. So you can change fear into anger very easily, and anger into fear—very easily.

Sometimes people come to me and they say, "We are feeling very afraid."

I tell them, "You go and beat a pillow and be angry with the pillow."

They say, "What will that do?"

I say, "You just try!" And it becomes a revelation to them. If they can beat the pillow in real, hot anger, immediately their fear disappears, because the same energy turns and becomes active. It was inactive, then it was fear.

Fear is the root cause of hate, anger, violence.

With such a small life, with such a small energy source, it is simply stupid to waste it in sadness, in anger, in hatred, in jealousy. Use it in love, use it in some creative act, use it in friendship, use it in meditation. Do something with your energy that takes you higher. And the higher you go, the more energy sources become available to you. At the highest point of consciousness, you are almost a god. ▩

This is the difference between negative and positive emotions: If you become aware of a certain emotion, and by your becoming aware the emotion dissolves, it is negative. If by your becoming aware of a certain emotion you then become the emotion, if the emotion then spreads and becomes your being, it is positive. Awareness works differently in each case. If it is a poisonous emotion, you are relieved of it through awareness. If it is good, blissful, ecstatic, you become one with it. Awareness deepens it.

So to me, this is the criterion: If something is deepened by your awareness, it is something good. If something is dissolved through awareness, it is something bad. That which cannot remain in awareness is sin and that which grows in awareness is virtue. Virtue and sin are not social concepts, they are inner realizations. ▦

Awareness is needed, not condemnation—and through awareness, transformation happens spontaneously. If you become aware of your anger, understanding penetrates. Just watching, with no judgment, not saying good, not saying bad, just watching in your inner sky. There is lightning, anger, you feel hot, the whole nervous system shaking and quaking, and you feel a tremor all over the body—a beautiful moment, because when energy functions you can watch it easily; when it is not functioning you cannot watch.

Close your eyes and meditate on it. Don't fight, just look at what is happening—the whole sky filled with electricity, so much lightning, so much beauty—just lie down on the ground and look at the sky and watch.

Then do the same inside. Clouds are there, because without clouds there can be no lightning—dark clouds are there, thoughts. Somebody has insulted you, somebody has laughed at you, somebody has said this or that...many clouds, dark clouds in the inner sky and much lightning. Watch! It is a beautiful scene—terrible also, because you don't understand. It is mysterious, and if mystery is not understood it becomes terrible, you are afraid of it.

And whenever a mystery is understood, it becomes a grace, a gift, because now you have the keys—and with keys you are the master. You don't "control" it—when you are aware, you simply become a master. ▣

A person who never becomes angry and who goes on controlling his anger is very dangerous. Beware of him; he can kill you. If your friend never becomes angry, report him to the police! A person who sometimes becomes angry is just a natural human being, there is no need to be concerned about it. But someone who never becomes angry will one day suddenly jump and strangle you! And he will do it as if he is possessed by something. Murderers have been telling the courts down through the ages, "I committed the crime, but I was possessed."

Who possessed them? Their own unconscious, their repressed unconscious, exploded. ▦

AT WAR

You never see animals going to war. Of course there are fights sometimes, but they are individual fights—not world wars with all the crows of the east fighting with all the crows of the west, or all the dogs of India fighting all the dogs of Pakistan. It is not. Dogs are not so foolish; neither are crows. Yes, sometimes they fight, and there is nothing wrong in it. If their freedom is violated, they fight. But the fight is individual, it is not a major war.

Now what have you done? You have repressed humanity and you have not allowed individuals to be angry sometimes, which is natural. The ultimate, total result is that everybody goes on gathering his anger, goes on repressing the anger; then one day everybody is so full of poison that it explodes into a world war. ▓

Obedience needs no intelligence. All machines are obedient. Nobody has ever heard of a disobedient machine. Obedience is simple too. It takes the burden of any responsibility off you. There is no need to react, you have simply to do what is being said. The responsibility rests with the source from where the order comes. In a certain way you are very free: You cannot be condemned for your act. ▧

The power is in such people's hands...any crackpot can push a button and finish off the whole of humanity, the whole of life on the earth. But perhaps deep down, humanity also wants to get rid of it. Perhaps individually they are not courageous enough to commit suicide, but on the mass scale they are ready.

Always remember, individuals have not committed great crimes. It is always crowds that commit great crimes, because in a crowd no individual feels, "I am responsible for what is happening." He thinks, "I am just being with the other people." Individually when you commit something, you have to think three times before committing it. What are you doing? Is it right? Does your consciousness permit it? But not when there is a crowd. You can be lost in the crowd, nobody will ever discover that you were also part of it.

The religions, the society, the politicians, have given people only fictions to live by. Now all those fictions are broken and people have nothing left to live for—hence their anguish. Anguish is not an ordinary state of anxiety. Anxiety is always centered upon a certain problem. You don't have money, you don't have enough clothes and the cold is coming, you are sick and you don't have medicine, and there is anxiety. Anxiety is about a certain problem.

Anguish has no problem as such. Just to be seems to *be* fruitless, futile. Just to breathe seems to be dragging yourself unnecessarily. You go on projecting for tomorrow—a moment comes when you start realizing that nothing is going to happen. Then there is anguish. In anguish, the only concern becomes somehow to get out of this circle of life—hence the increasing rate of suicide, and an unconscious desire of humanity that the third world war happens, so..."I am not responsible that I committed suicide. The world war killed everybody, and killed me too." ▨

What is the need of nations?

The whole earth is one.

Only on the maps do you go on drawing lines, and over those lines you go on fighting and killing and murdering. It is such a stupid game that unless the whole of humanity is mad, it is impossible to think how it continues. ▨

POWER TRIP

You need power only to do something harmful.

Otherwise love is enough, compassion is enough. ▨

There can be no political revolution, no social revolution, no economic revolution. The only revolution is that of the spirit; it is individual. And if millions of individuals change, then the society will change as a consequence, not vice versa. You cannot change the society first and hope that individuals will change later on. ▨

Political power is ugly. Power over others is ugly. It is inhuman, because to have power over somebody means to reduce that person to a thing. He becomes your possession. ▦

What politicians have been doing all over the world, all through history, is simply inhuman and ugly. But the reason, the basic reason is that they have a deep feeling of inferiority and they want to prove to themselves that it is not so. "Look, you have so much power, so many people in your hands that you can make or break, so many nuclear weapons. Just push a button and you can destroy the whole planet."

Power over others is destructive—always destructive. In a better world, anybody who is ambitious, who wants to be more important than others, who wants to be ahead of others, should be treated psychologically. ▣

The real history has not yet been written because we become too engrossed in the temporal things. We become too obsessed with the newspaper, which is only relevant today and tomorrow will be meaningless.

If you have eyes to see, see the point: Become interested in the eternal. ▣

THE LANGUAGE OF CELEBRATION

We are taught that unless there is recognition we are nobody, we are worthless. The work is not important, but the recognition. And this is putting things upside down. The work should be important—a joy in itself. You should work not to be recognized but because you enjoy being creative; you love the work for its own sake. Work at something because you love it. Don't ask for recognition. If it comes, take it easily; if it does not come, don't think about it. Your fulfillment should be in the work itself. And if everybody learns this simple art of loving his work, whatever it is, enjoying it without asking for any recognition, we will have a more beautiful and celebrating world. ▩

Existence is abundant—millions and millions of flowers, millions of birds, millions of animals—everything in abundance. Nature is not ascetic, it is dancing everywhere—in the ocean, in the trees. It is singing everywhere—in the wind passing through the pine trees, in the birds....What is the need of millions of galaxies, of each galaxy having millions of stars? There seems to be no need, except that abundance is the very nature of existence; that richness is the very core. Existence does not believe in poverty. ▨

If you know how to enjoy a rose flower, a green tree in your courtyard, the mountains, the river, the stars, the moon, if you know how to enjoy people, you will not be obsessed with money. The obsession is arising because we have forgotten the language of celebration.

I will not tell you to renounce money. That has been told to you down the ages; it has not changed you. I am going to tell you something else: Celebrate life, and the obsession with money disappears automatically. And when it goes on its own accord, it leaves no mark, it leaves no wounds, it leaves no trace behind. ▨

Buffaloes don't make parties to revolutionize the world, to change buffaloes into super-buffaloes, to make buffaloes religious, virtuous. No animal is concerned at all with human ideas. And they must all be laughing: "What has happened to you? Why can't you just be yourself as you are? What is the need to be somebody else?" ▩

Life in itself is an empty canvas, it becomes whatsoever you paint on it. You can paint misery, you can paint bliss. This freedom is your glory. ▨

Nobody is superior, nobody is inferior, but nobody is equal either. People are simply unique, incomparable.

You are you, I am me. I have to contribute my potential to life; you have to contribute your potential to life.

I have to discover my own being; you have to discover your own being. ▩

When you see anger in others, go and dig within yourself and you will find it there; when you see too much ego in others, just go inside and you will find ego sitting there. The inside functions like a projector; others become screens and you start seeing films projected on others that are really your own tapes. ▦

Whenever there is joy, you feel it is coming from without. You have met a friend—of course, it appears that the joy is coming from your friend, from seeing him. That is not the actual case. The joy is always within you; the friend has just become a provocation. The friend has helped it to come out, has helped you to see that the joy is there.

And this is not only with joy, but with everything: With anger, with sadness, with misery, with happiness, with everything it is so. Others are only providing situations where things that are hidden within you can be expressed. They are not the causes; they are not causing something in you. Whatsoever is happening, is happening to *you*. It has always been there; it is only that meeting with this friend has become a situation in which whatsoever was hidden has come out in the open. From the hidden sources it has become apparent, manifest.

Whenever this happens, remain centered in the inner feeling and then you will have a different attitude about everything in life. ▦

Once pathology disappears, everybody becomes a creator. Let it be understood as deeply as possible: Only ill people are destructive. The people who are healthy are creative. Creativity is a kind of fragrance of real health. When a person is really healthy and whole, creativity comes naturally; the urge to create arises.

When you don't compare, when you don't compete, when you are not ambitious, when you don't want to be anybody other than who you are, you accumulate much energy—because all that energy that was being wasted in competition and conflict is no longer wasted. You become a reservoir. Out of that energy comes creativity.

Creativity has nothing to do with competition, it has something to do with overflowing energy. William Blake is right when he says, "Energy is delight." When you are overflowing with energy, aglow with energy, aflame with energy, the energy itself becomes creativity. You start growing, but now the growth has a totally different connotation. It has no goal—it has a source but no goal. Now you are not thinking what to be; you are not following a particular goal, a particular plan. You are such a big river that through your rushing energy you will reach the ocean. No river is searching for the ocean, but rivers reach the ocean;

and no river is competing with any other river, but all rivers reach the ocean. The river reaches the ocean through overflowing water. That very energy is enough to take it to the ocean.

You can become an ocean of creativity if you are contented. Then creativity arises in you, grows in you—not for any ideal, but just because you have too much: You have to share it. You have to sing a song, because the heart is so full and overflowing that you have to pour it into songs. You cannot contain the energy, hence the overflow happens. That overflow is creativity. ▨

ALWAYS A RIVER

"Relationship" means something complete, finished, closed. Love is never a relationship; love is relating. It is always a river, flowing, unending. Love knows no full stop; the honeymoon begins but never ends. Lovers end, love continues. It is a continuum. It is a verb, not a noun.

And why do we reduce the beauty of relating to relationship? Why are we in such a hurry?—because to relate is insecure and relationship is a form of security. "Relationship" has a certainty. Relating is just a meeting of two strangers, maybe just an overnight stay and in the morning we say good-bye; who knows what is going to happen tomorrow? ▩

Love is not a quantity, it is a quality—and a quality of a certain category that grows by giving and dies if you hold it. If you are miserly about it, it dies. So be really spendthrift! Be free with giving your love. ▦

Love knows how to go into the unknown. Love knows how to throw aside all securities. Love knows how to move into the unfamiliar and the uncharted. Love is courage. Trust love. ▣

THE REAL THING

I am against plastic flowers. Real flowers are very different. Plastic flowers are permanent—plastic love will be permanent. The real flower is not permanent, it is changing moment to moment. Today it is there dancing in the wind and in the sun and in the rain. Tomorrow you will not be able to find it—it has disappeared just as mysteriously as it had appeared.

Real love is like a real flower. ▦

Ordinarily, in your dictionaries you will find "permanent" as if it is a synonym for "eternal." It is not. The eternal is always momentary. Look at the rose flower again. In the morning it is there; by the evening it is gone. It was momentary. But it will come again—tomorrow in the morning another rose is there. It has always been coming. The eternal emerges through the momentary, the eternal looks through the momentary. One flower goes, another flower comes; that goes, another is coming; in fact, the one goes just to make place for the other. The beauty is eternal. The "roseness" is eternal. Rose flowers come and go; the roseness is eternal.

Live in the momentary. And live in the momentary without any desire for the permanent; otherwise you will miss the eternal. Live in the moment so tremendously and totally that you forget the permanent. The permanent is a projection in the future; the permanent is your desire. It has nothing to do with reality. The eternal is the depth of the momentary—the eternal is in the moment. The permanent is horizontal, linear. The eternal is vertical.

Somebody is swimming on the surface of a deep river; that's how the permanent is. And somebody dives deep in the river; that's how the eternal is. Dive deep in the moment and you will touch the eternal. Look in the rose flower. Yes, this rose flower is momentary, but look deep, dive deep, and suddenly you will see that hidden behind this rose flower is roseness. Hidden behind this momentary rose flower is beauty eternal, divine. Flowers will come and go; flowering remains. Roses come and go; roseness remains. Lovers come and go; love remains. ▣

The one who knows how to live knows how to die. The one who knows how to fall in love knows when the moment has come to fall out of it. He falls out of it gracefully, with a good-bye, with gratitude.

People don't know how to love, and then they don't know how to say good-bye when the time has come to say it. If you love you will know that everything begins and everything ends, and there is a time for beginning and there is a time for ending, and there is no wound in it. One is not wounded, one simply knows the season is over. One is not in despair, one simply understands, and one thanks the other, "You gave me so many beautiful gifts. You gave me new visions of life, you opened a few windows I might never have opened on my own. Now the time has come that we separate and our ways part." Not in anger, not in rage, not with a grudge, not with any complaint, but with tremendous gratitude, with great love, with thankfulness in the heart. ▨

IN WONDER

Only blind people believe in light. Those who have eyes don't believe in light, they simply see it.

Truth needs meditative eyes. If you don't have meditative eyes, then the whole of life is just dull dead facts, unrelated to each other, accidental, meaningless, a jumble, just a chance phenomenon.

If you see the truth, everything falls into line. Everything falls together in a harmony, everything starts having significance.

Remember always, significance is the shadow of truth. And those who live only in facts live an utterly meaningless life. ▨

Truth cannot be transferred. Truth cannot be handed over to you by somebody else, because it is not a commodity. It is not a thing, it is an experience. ▣

I do not believe in believing. That has to be understood first.

Nobody asks me, "Do you believe in the rose flower?" There is no need. You can see; the rose flower is there or it is not there. Only fictions, not facts, have to be believed.

Belief is comfortable, convenient; it dulls. It is a kind of drug; it makes you a zombie.

A zombie can be a Christian, Hindu, Mohammedan—but they are all zombies, with different labels. And sometimes they get fed up with one label, so they change the label: The Hindu becomes a Christian, the Christian becomes a Hindu—a new label, a fresh label, but behind the label the same belief system.

Destroy your beliefs. Certainly it will be uncomfortable, inconvenient, but nothing valuable is ever gained without inconvenience. 🀫

Theists and atheists both are victims. The really religious person has nothing to do with the Bible or the Koran or the Bhagavad Gita. The really religious person has a deep communion with existence. He can say yes to a rose flower, he can say yes to the stars, he can say yes to people. He can say yes to his own being, to his own desires. He can say yes to whatsoever life brings to him. ▣

Religion is not something to be believed in, but something to be lived, something to be experienced. It is not a belief in your mind but the flavor of your whole being. ▨

The word "religion" has to be understood. The word is significant: It means putting the parts together so that the parts are no longer parts, but become whole. The root meaning of the word "religion" is to put things together in such a way that the part is no longer a part, but becomes the whole.

Each part becomes the whole, in togetherness.

Each part, separate, is dead. Joined together, a new quality appears— the quality of the whole. And to bring that quality into your life is the purpose of religion.

It has nothing to do with God or the devil. But the way the religions have functioned in the world, they have changed its whole quality, the very fabric. Instead of making it a science of integration, so that man is not many, but one, the religions around the world have helped humanity to forget even the meaning of the word. ▣

Looking at a sunset, just for a second you forget your separateness and you *are* the sunset. That is the moment when you feel the beauty of it. But the moment you say that it is a "beautiful sunset," you are no longer feeling it; you have come back to your separate, enclosed entity of the ego. Now the mind is speaking. And this is one of the mysteries— that the mind can speak, and knows nothing; and the heart knows everything, and cannot speak. ▣

It is the most beautiful moment in one's life when there is neither confusion nor certainty. One simply is, a mirror reflecting that which is, with no direction, going nowhere, with no idea of doing something, with no future, just utterly in the moment, tremendously in the moment. ▨

The knowable is ordinary, mundane. The unknowable is sacred. And only with the unknowable does life become a benediction, only with the unknowable are you thrilled with the wonder of life and existence. ▨

Knowledge gratifies the ego, wisdom happens only when the ego is gone, forgotten. Knowledge can be taught; universities exist to teach you. Wisdom cannot be taught, it is like an infection: You have to be with the wise, you have to move with the wise, and only then will something start moving inside you. ▨

When you are able to see with no dust of knowledge on the mirror of your soul, when your soul is without any dust of knowledge, when it is just a mirror, it reflects that which is. That is wisdom. That reflecting of that which is, is wisdom. ▩

Whenever you laugh you are close to the divine, whenever you love you are close to the divine. Whenever you sing and dance and make music, that is what real religion is. ▓

Wisdom has nothing to do with knowledge, not at all; it has something to do with innocence. Something of the purity of the heart is a must, something of the spaciousness of being is needed for wisdom to grow. ▓

Be in a state of not knowing; function from that state. Look at trees like a child, look at the moon like a poet, look at the sky like a madman! ▦

Remain in wonder if you want the mysteries to open up for you. Mysteries never open up for those who go on questioning. Questioners sooner or later end up in a library. Questioners sooner or later end up with scriptures, because scriptures are full of answers. And answers are dangerous, they kill your wonder.

They are dangerous because they give you the feeling that you know, although you know not. They give you this misconception about yourself that now questions have been solved. "I know what the Bible says, I know what the Koran says, I know what the Gita says. I have arrived." You will become a parrot; you will repeat things but you will not know anything. This is not the way to know—knowledge is not the way to know.

Then what is the way to know? Wonder. Let your heart dance with wonder. Be full of wonder: Throb with it, breathe it in, breathe it out. Why be in such a hurry for the answer? Can't you allow a mystery to remain a mystery? I know there is a great temptation not to allow it to remain a mystery, to reduce it to knowledge. Why is this temptation there?—because only if you are full of knowledge will you be in control.

Mystery will control you, knowledge will make you the controller. Mystery will possess you. You cannot possess the mysterious; it is so vast and your hands are so small. It is so infinite, you cannot possess it, you will have to be possessed by it—and that is the fear. Knowledge you can possess, it is so trivial; knowledge you can control.

This temptation of the mind to reduce every wonder, every mystery, to a question, is basically fear-oriented. We are afraid, afraid of the tremendousness of life, of this incredible existence. We are afraid. Out of fear we create some small knowledge around ourselves as a protection, as an armor, as a defense.

It is only cowards who reduce the tremendously valuable capacity of wondering to questions. The really brave, the courageous person, leaves it as it is. Rather than changing it into a question, he jumps into the mystery. Rather than trying to control it, he allows the mystery to possess him. ▨

From the state of wonder, there are two paths. One is of questioning—
the wrong path—it leads you into more and more knowledge. The
other is not of questioning but enjoying. Enjoy the wonder, the wonder
that life is, the wonder that existence is, the wonder of the sun and the
sunlight and the trees bathed in its golden rays.

Experience it. Don't put a question mark on it, let it be as it is. ▦

Life is its own purpose; it is not a means to some end, it is an end unto itself. The bird on the wing, the rose in the wind, the sun rising in the morning, the stars in the night, a man falling in love with a woman, a child playing on the street...there is no purpose. Life is simply enjoying itself, delighting in itself. Energy is overflowing, dancing, for no purpose at all. ▦

They say art is for art's sake. It may be so, it may not be so—I am not an artist. But I can say to you: Life is for life's sake. Each moment is utterly for its own sake. To sacrifice it for anything else is unintelligent. And once the habit of sacrificing settles, then you will sacrifice this moment for the next, and the next for the next, and so on, so forth—this year for the next year, and this life for the next life! It is a simple, logical process: Once you have taken the first step, then the whole journey starts— the journey that leads you into the wasteland, the journey that is self-destructive, suicidal.

Live in the moment for the sheer joy of living it. Live with no should, with no ought, with no must, with no commandment. You are not here to be a martyr, you are here to enjoy life to its fullest.

And the only way to live, love, enjoy, is to forget the future. It exists not. If you can forget the future, if you can see that it is not there, there is no point in constantly getting ready for it. The moment the future is dropped, the past becomes irrelevant on its own. We carry the past so that we can use it in the future. Otherwise who will carry the past?

It is unnecessary. If there is no future, what is the point of carrying the knowledge that the past has given to you? It is a burden that will destroy the joy of the journey.

And let me remind you, it is a pure journey. Life is a pilgrimage to nowhere—from nowhere to nowhere. And between these two nowheres is the now-here. Nowhere consists of two words: *now, here*. Between these two nowheres is the now-here. ▓

THE END OF THE ROAD

To know that all has failed is the beginning of a new journey. To know that "All that I have achieved is lost" is the beginning of a new search for something that cannot be lost. When one is utterly disillusioned with the world and all its successes, only then does one become spiritual.

A poor man is never so poor because still he has hopes: Some day or other, destiny is going to shower blessings on him; some day or other he will be able to arrive, to achieve. He can hope. The rich man has arrived, his hopes are fulfilled—now, suddenly, he finds nothing is fulfilled. All hopes fulfilled, and yet nothing is fulfilled. He has arrived and he has not arrived at all—it has always been a dream journey. He has not moved a single inch.

A man who is successful in the world feels the pain of being a failure as nobody else can feel it. There is a proverb that says that nothing succeeds like success. I would like to tell you: Nothing fails like success.

But you cannot know it unless you have succeeded. When all the riches are there that you have dreamed about, planned about, worked hard for, then sitting just amidst those riches is the beggar—deep inside empty, hollow; nothing inside, everything outside.

In fact, when everything is there outside, it becomes a contrast. It simply emphasizes your inner emptiness and nothingness. It simply emphasizes your inner beggarliness, poverty. A rich man knows poverty as no poor man can ever know. ▨

It is so cheap to become knowledgeable. Scriptures are there; libraries are there, universities are there; it is so easy to become knowledgeable. And once you become knowledgeable you are in a very sensitive space, because the ego would like to believe that this is your knowledge— not only knowledgeability, it is your wisdom. The ego would like to change knowledge into wisdom. You will start believing that you know.

You know nothing. You know only books and what is written in books. Perhaps those books are written by persons just like you.

Ninety-nine percent of books are written by other bookish people. In fact, if you read ten books, your mind becomes so full of rubbish that you would like to pour it down into the eleventh book. What else are you going to do with it? You have to unburden yourself. ▣

Inquiry is a risk. It is moving into the unknown. One knows not what is going to happen.

One leaves everything that one is acquainted with, is comfortable with, and moves into the unknown, not even perfectly certain whether there is anything on the other shore, or even whether there *is* the other shore.

So people cling either to theism, or those who are a little stronger, intellectual, the intelligentsia—they cling to atheism. But both are escapes from the doubt. And to escape from doubt is to escape from inquiry—because what is doubt? It is only a question mark. It is not your enemy, it is simply a question mark within you which prepares you to inquire.

Doubt is your friend. ▦

AFTERWORD

Intrigued?

These thoughtful little books may also be of interest to you:

Awareness: The Key to Living in Balance

Courage: The Joy of Living Dangerously

Creativity: Unleashing the Forces Within

Intimacy: Trusting Oneself and the Other

Intuition: Knowing Beyond Logic

Maturity: The Responsibility of Being Oneself

ABOUT THE AUTHOR

Osho is one of the best known and most provocative spiritual teachers of our time. Beginning in the 1970s, he captured the attention of young people in the West who wanted to experience meditation and transformation. More than a decade after his death in 1990, the influence of his teachings continues to expand, reaching seekers of all ages in virtually every country of the world. Osho's works challenge readers to examine and break free of their conditioned belief systems and prejudices, which limit their capacity to enjoy life in all its richness.